Stage 1

Car Thieves

**Longman
Structural
Readers**

L. G. Alexander

Illustrated by
D. G. Grant

Part One

It is morning. Two thieves are standing near a big building. Their names are Conway and Page. The thieves are watching the cars.

A big red car stops in front of the building and a man leaves the car. The man is going into the building. The thieves are watching him, but he does not see them.

The man is in the building and the thieves run to the car. "Quick, Page!" Conway shouts. "The door of the car is open. The keys are in the car, too." "The keys!" Page shouts. "We're lucky this morning."

  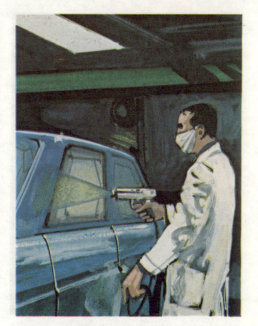

"Be quick!" Conway shouts. "Drive to Denny's Garage. This is an expensive car. We can sell the car to Denny. This is our lucky morning."
"Yes," Page answers. "Denny can buy the car from us."

The car leaves. The thieves drive to Denny's Garage. "Drive into the garage and stop the car," Conway says. "Then give the keys to me."

This is Denny Young. He is a clever man. He buys cars from thieves. He changes the engine number and the licence number. Then he paints the cars and sells them. Denny is busy now. He is painting a car.

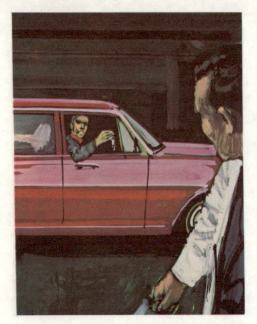  

"Hullo, Denny!" Page shouts.
"Hullo," Denny answers. "I'm busy. What do you want?"
"Here's a new car for you," Page answers. "It's an expensive car. Here are the keys. Come and look at it. We want £500 for this car."

Denny Young looks at the car and laughs. "Yes, it's a nice car," he says. "I can change the engine number and the licence number. Then I can paint it and sell it. Come and see me tomorrow. I can't give you £500, but I can give you £400."

Conway is looking in the car. "Look!" he calls. "Here's a camera. It's an expensive camera, too!"
"Perhaps I can buy that, too," Denny says.
The thieves laugh.

  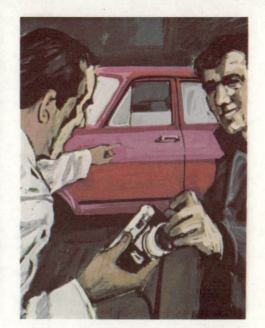

"Is it a good camera?" Page asks.
"Take a photograph, Conway," Denny calls.
Conway takes a photograph of Denny and Page. "That's a nice picture," Conway says.

"Give the camera to me," Denny says. He looks at it. "Yes, it is a nice camera."
"Take my photograph now," Conway calls.
Conway sits on the car and Denny takes his photograph.

"Here, Conway," Denny calls. "Take this camera and put it in the car. You are clever men. Come and see me tomorrow. I can give £400 to you for the car and £20 to you for the camera."

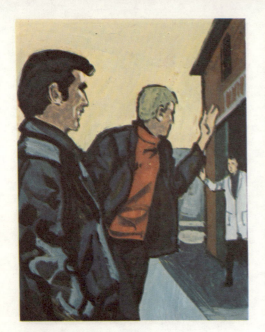  

"You can go now," Denny says, "and be quick. I'm busy this morning. Goodbye."
"Goodbye, Denny," the thieves say. They are laughing.
"It's our lucky day," Page says.

It is afternoon. The man leaves the building. He cannot see his car. "My car! My car!" he shouts. "I can't find my car!" A woman hears him. She stops and talks to him. "What is it?" the woman asks.

"I can't find my car," the man says. "It isn't here."
"Go to the police station," the woman answers. "The police station is near here. It is near that building."
"Thank you," the man says.

Part Two

The man is going into the police station. He is sad. He is going to talk to the police. He is going to talk to them about his car.

The man sees Inspector James Wood.
"Good afternoon, Inspector," the man says. "My name is John Read. I can't find my car."
"Sit here," the inspector says, "and describe the car."
"Thank you, Inspector."

John Read sits on a chair and the Inspector sits near his desk. John Read describes his car and the Inspector writes in a book.
"What is the licence number?" the Inspector asks.
"PQ 2475," John Read answers.

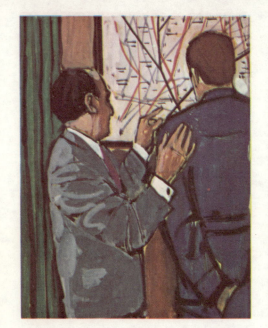  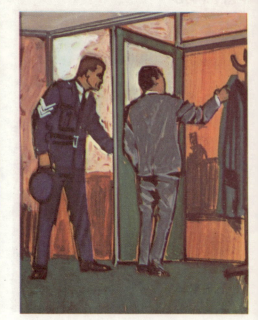

Now Inspector Wood is talking to a policeman. "Thieves take cars from this place," he says. "Ten cars this year. Denny Young buys these cars. I am sure of it. The car thieves take the cars to his garage. His garage is here."

"Can we arrest him, Inspector?" the policeman asks.
"No, we can't arrest him," the Inspector says. "He is clever. He buys the cars and paints them. Then he changes the licence number and the engine number. I am sure of that."

"We can't prove it," the policeman says.
"No, we can't prove it now, but we are going to prove it."
"What can we do?"
"I'm not sure, but we can go to his garage. Take me there now."

Inspector Wood and the policeman are going to Denny Young's Garage. The policeman is driving the car.
"What are you going to do?" the policeman asks. "I'm going to talk to Denny Young about that car," the Inspector says.

Denny sees the Inspector and the policeman. "Hullo, Inspector," he calls. "Are you busy?" "Of course I am," the Inspector answers. "You're busy, too." "Of course," Denny laughs. "This is a garage. What do you want?"

The Inspector does not answer. He looks at the car. "That's a nice car, Denny," he says. "Yes, Inspector," Denny answers. "Do you want to buy it? You can buy it for £1,000."

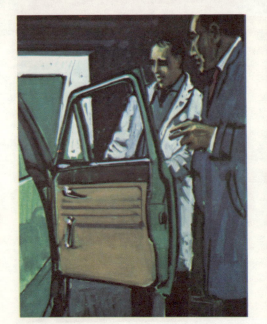

"No, thank you," Inspector Wood says. "It's an expensive car. Can I see it?"
"Of course, Inspector," Denny says.

The Inspector goes into the car. He looks at it.

Then the Inspector looks at the engine and talks to Denny. "Is this your car, Denny?"
"Yes," Denny answers, "but it's not a new car. I'm going to sell it. Two men want to buy it tomorrow, but I can sell it to you."

"We're going now, Denny," Inspector Wood says. "Goodbye, Inspector," Denny calls.

"That car doesn't belong to John Read," the policeman says. "Read's car is a different colour. It's red."
"It's a different colour, but it isn't a different car. That car belongs to Read. I am sure of it."
"But you can't prove it."

"Perhaps I can prove it tomorrow," the Inspector says. "A policeman can watch the garage. Two men are going to see Young tomorrow." "He's clever," the policeman says. "We can't arrest him." "Perhaps," the Inspector says.

Part Three

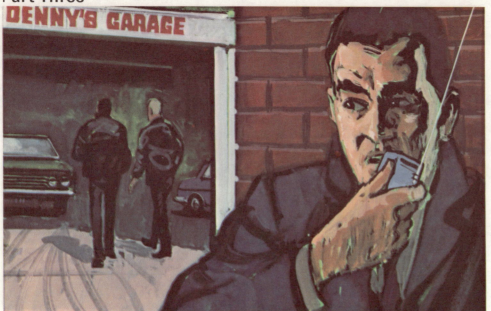

It is morning. The thieves are going to Denny's Garage. They want £420.

A policeman is watching them. "Hullo," the policeman says. "Is that Inspector Wood? Two men are going into Denny's Garage."

The thieves are in the garage. "Here is your £420," Denny says. "Is that the car?" they ask.

"Yes," Denny answers, "but it's a different colour now. The engine number is different and the licence number is different, too!"

A police car is going to Denny's Garage. Inspector Wood is in the car. He is with five policemen.

The thieves hear the police car. "What's that?" Conway asks. "It's the police," Denny laughs. "It's Inspector Wood. This isn't my car. The Inspector is sure of that, but he can't prove it!"

"Quick," Conway says. "We can run away."
"No, stay here," Denny says. "The police are going to ask questions. You can say, 'We are going to buy this car. We are going to buy it for £1,000'."

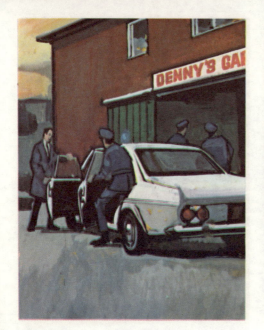  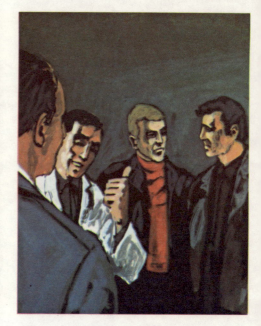

The police car stops near Denny's Garage.
"You stay in the car," Inspector Wood says. "You four men come with me."

The police go into the garage.
"Hullo, Inspector," Denny laughs.
"Hullo, Denny," the Inspector says. "Are you going to buy this car?" Denny asks.
"No, Denny," the Inspector says.

"That's good," Denny answers. "These men are my friends. They want to buy this car for £1,000."
"Yes," Page says. "We are going to buy this car."

"And I am going to arrest you," the Inspector says. "This isn't your car, Denny, and these two men aren't going to buy it. This car belongs to John Read. You men are car thieves, and you, Denny, are buying the car from them."

Denny hears the Inspector and laughs. "You can't arrest us," he shouts. "Describe Read's car, Inspector. This is a different car. You say, 'This car belongs to John Read'. Prove it! Prove it!"
"I can prove it," Inspector Wood answers.

"Can you see this camera? It belongs to John Read. I found it in the car. Can you see these photographs? They are photographs of you and of this car. Come with us and be quick. We are going to the police station."

Exercises

A. Read these sentences:
  He is taking my photograph.
  Take my photograph.
Now change these sentences:
1. He is giving the camera to me.
2. He is selling the car.
3. He is changing the licence number.
4. He is putting the camera in the car.
5. He is talking to her.
6. He is sitting on that chair.
7. He is arresting these men.

B. Read this sentence:
  We can prove it and **we are going to prove it**.
Now finish these sentences:
1. I can sell it and _____.
2. She can change it and _____.
3. They can buy it and _____.
4. He can paint it and _____.
5. We can look at it and _____.
6. I can take it and _____.

C. Read these sentences:
  We **cannot** arrest him.
We can say:
  We **can't** arrest him.
Now change the words in these sentences:
1. **I am** sure of it.
2. **It is** an expensive car.
3. **Here is** a camera.
4. It **is not** here.
5. I **cannot** find my car.

D. Read these sentences:
  This is our car.
  Denny can buy it **from us**.
Now finish these sentences:
1. This is my car. Denny can buy it _____.
2. This is her car. Denny can buy it _____.
3. This is their car. Denny can buy it _____.
4. This is his car. Denny can buy it _____.
5. This is our car. Denny can buy it _____.

E. Read these sentences:
  Look at that man.
  He is going to leave the building.
Now finish these sentences:
1. Look at that woman. _____ is going to talk to him.
2. Look at that camera. _____ is an expensive camera.
3. Look at those thieves. _____ are going to take the car.
4. Look at that policeman. _____ is going to arrest the thief.
5. Look at that dog. _____ is black and white.